Chicks
Don't Eat
Candy!

D1736621

Kelly Tills

A division of FDI publishing LLC

The delightful thing
about baby chicks is...

chicks don't eat
candy!

People eat candy. Ants eat candy off the ground.

Even cows can eat candy
(but they like grass better).

Do chicks eat donuts?

No!
Donuts are people food.

Do chicks eat
pancakes?

No!
Pancakes are people food, too

Do chicks eat worms?

Yes! Chicks love to eat worms.

So why
don't chicks eat
candy?

Tongues are for tasting.
There are lots of bumps you
can see on tongues.

Inside those bumps
are even tinier bumps
you can't see.

Those are taste buds.

There are different taste buds for tasting different flavors.

There are
salty taste buds,

savory taste buds,

sour taste buds,

and sweet taste buds.

Chicks don't have taste buds
for sweet stuff.

Do kids have taste buds for

sweet stuff?

Definitely.

Mother hens teach chicks what
is healthy to eat.
Just like people do.

Except mother hens don't have to worry about chicks sneaking candy under the table.

But chicks might sneak some

extra worms,

or some

spaghetti,

or
spaghetti
worms!

That's the
delightful thing
about baby chicks.

What's a
delightful thing
about
you?

Well, actually...

people have thousands of taste buds, but chicks only have a few hundred. We can taste a LOT more flavors than they can.

Whoa! That's crazy.